There are certain people who can
bring us a ray of happiness
with just a smile
and who can make us feel better
just by listening and showing
that they care...
These special kinds of friends are
treasured within the heart and are
a part of our souls

— Shannon M. Lester

True Friends
Always Remain in Each Other's Heart

*A Blue Mountain Arts®
Collection*

Edited by Gary Morris

Blue Mountain Press™

SPS Studios, Inc., Boulder, Colorado

We wish to thank Susan Polis Schutz for permission to reprint the following poems tha:
appear in this publication: "True Friends," "A Thought for a Wonderful Friend," and "I Car
Wait to Be with You Again, My Friend." Copyright © 1983, 1988, 1989 by Stephen Schui
and Susan Polis Schutz. All rights reserved.

Library of Congress Catalog Card Number: 2001002871
ISBN: 0-88396-277-2

ACKNOWLEDGMENTS appear on page 64.

Certain trademarks are used under license.

Manufactured in the United States of America.
Third printing of this edition: 2003

❀ This book is printed on recycled paper.
This book is printed on fine quality, laid embossed, 80 lb. paper. This paper has been
specially produced to be acid free (neutral pH) and contains no groundwood or
unbleached pulp. It conforms with all the requirements of the American National
Standards Institute, Inc., so as to ensure that this book will last and be enjoyed by future
generations.

Library of Congress Cataloging-in-Publication Data

True friends always remain in each other's heart : a Blue Mountain Arts collection.
   p. cm.
  ISBN 0-88396-277-2 (softcover : alk. paper)
  1. Friendship—Poetry. 2. American poetry.
  PS595.F74 T78 2001
  811.008'0353—dc21

                              2001002871
                                CIP

SPS Studios, Inc.
P.O. Box 4549, Boulder, Colorado 80306

Contents

Ours Is a Lifelong Friendship

In this chaotic world where it seems we constantly race to catch today, an enduring friendship such as ours didn't just happen — we built it moment by moment, year upon year, with understanding and sacrifice, care and trust, tears and love.

I wish I could discover new words to tell you how deeply thankful I am for your never-ending friendship. But some feelings are not meant for words; some feelings are more eloquently expressed silently, heart to heart, soul to soul.

Although our life journeys sometimes take us far apart and down different paths, when your life changes, so does mine. I believe our willingness to encourage and embrace the changing aspects of each other's life continually strengthens and renews our special bond.

You are the truest friend I have ever known. Whatever courses our lives take, always remember that there will never be a day that I do not think of you, pray for you, and send you my love.

May happiness beyond measure and love without end grace every corner of your life... forever and always.

— E. M. Uso

Our Friendship Is a Wonderful Part of My Days

Our friendship has always been
   the kind that lets us talk
and tell each other anything.
We've always gathered our thoughts
   and feelings
and laid them at each other's doorstep.

As friends, we've shared a million
   memories —
some sad and many happy ones.
We've opened those special places
   in the heart
where only best friends are welcome.
We've been through thick and thin
   together.

We've done our best to bring hope
    to each other
when it looked like all hope was gone.
We've cheered each other on until
    a tiny smile was born.

We've always been open and honest
    with each other;
we've had the kind of friendship
    that most people never find.

What I'm trying to say is this:
As long as you have me
    and I have you for a friend,
life's never going to be
    lonely, boring,
or without someone special
    in our lives.
Our friendship means so much
    to me.

— Barbara J. Hall

A Friend
Is a Part of You Always

Friendship is a special gift
given to us all.
The smile of a friend
is sunlight on a cloudy day,
and every smile given to a friend
is returned.

A friend is one whom you can talk to
    and listen to without judging.
A friend doesn't ignore your faults,
but accepts them as a part of you.
A friend is a shoulder to lean on
    when you need support,
a pat on the back when you do well,
and a sympathetic ear when you fail.
A friend is a person you can laugh with
    about everything,
you can cry with without shame,
and whom you trust completely.
A friend is a partner in life
    and a part of you always.

— Brian Bindschadler

Let's Never Let Go of Our Friendship

I don't ever want us to let go
of each other.
Maybe our paths will go
in separate directions,
but that won't change the bond
we share and what's in our hearts.

No matter where I am
or what I am doing,
when you come to mind
a smile comes to my face
and a warmth settles in my heart.

The day you and I met
will always be cherished.
We've grown together,
done a lot together,

and no matter what,
we always let each other know
that we do love and care
about each other.
You are more than just
   a friend to me.

I often struggle to say how I feel,
but I hope we never let go
of what we share,
because whether it's across the miles
or just a short distance,
you are and will always be
a part of my life and me.

— Betsy Gurganus

A Thought
for a Wonderful Friend

Sometimes we are lucky enough
to meet a person
who stands out
among all the other people
as being extremely special
who knows what we
are thinking about
who is happy for us at all times
who is always there to talk to us
who cares about us selflessly
who is always truthful with us
Sometimes we are lucky enough
to meet someone who is
extremely wonderful
For me
that person
is you
my dear friend

— Susan Polis Schutz

You Are the Best Friend
I've Ever Known

You are my best friend.
You listen to what I have to say,
no matter how unimportant.
You listen without judging;
you give your opinion when asked.
You listen wholeheartedly,
without distractions.

You are my best friend.
You care about me,
about who I am,
where I am going,
what I am doing.
You care about our relationship
and make that extra effort
to make me feel at home with you.

We complement and complete
   each other.
You give so much of yourself
to me and to others,
without ever expecting
   more in return.

You are my best friend,
and you'll always be
a part of my life.

— Barbara Carlson

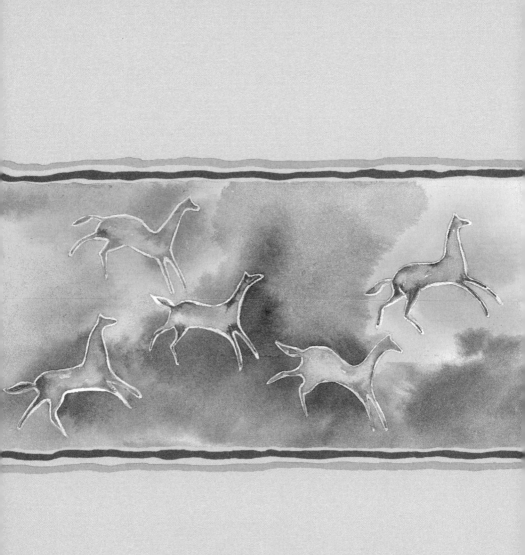

I'll Always Be There
and I'll Always Care;
I'll Always Be Your Friend

There are a thousand things
I would like to be for you...
but one of the most important
is just being
the someone
you can talk to.

There are so many things
I would like
to do for you...
and so many things I would like
to say and give and share.

But for today
I just want you to know
that I promise to be
your friend for life.

I'll always be there,
and I'll always care.

— A. Rogers

There's Distance Between Us, My Friend, but I'm Always Just a Thought Away

There's distance between us
these days, my friend,
distance and a little ache
for the days when we were
right there
to share laughter and tears,
to listen and be listened to.
Now the space between us
makes that hard, and yet,
tried and true friendships are rare
and not often found,
and yours is one
I want with all my heart to keep.

Though there is physical distance
between us,
there is a place inside me
where thoughts of you
are kept warm and safe,
and there are times
when I still smile,
thinking of what we've shared.
Remember, my friend,
if you want or need me,
I'm a phone call, a letter,
or a thought away.
If I can help, let me know,
for a true friend
remains a friend
now and for always.

— Ruthann Tholen

My Friend,
We Share a Special Bond

It is so very hard
to find someone in your life
that you can become close to
and friends with.
It takes a special bond
to bring two people together —
a lot of patience
and understanding,
a sprinkle of mischief for
    the good times,
and an abundance of laughter.
If you're lucky,
you find someone you can love,
someone who is
what you have been to me —
my best friend.

— Nanci Brillant

Our Friendship Is a Wonderful Feeling That I Carry in My Heart

Because of who you are,
   we're friends.
Whether it was your smile
   or your laugh
   that caught my eye,
it was definitely your
   concerned attitude
   that captured my heart.
When we first met, I felt like
   I had known you all my life.
I could talk to you so easily;
I could trust you with my
   innermost thoughts;
I could laugh with you on
   the spur of the moment.

With you, I don't have to pretend
    to be anything I'm not.
You accept me for who I am and what
    I represent.
You are that rare kind of person
    who cares enough to allow
    and even encourage a person to be
    who they are.
You have helped me through
    what could have been difficult times.
"Thanks" just doesn't adequately
    express my appreciation.
But even more than that,
I appreciate your friendship.
It is one that rises from our hearts
    and will always be cherished.

— Rita Rider

Ｙou're one of the
closest friends I've got.

And I want you to know that
for all we've been through,
all the sharing, the encouragement,
the serious and the silly times
and the just-being-together times,
I've come to appreciate you so much.

Whenever I think of you,
I think of a very special friend
who makes my world a better place to be.
And this seemed like the perfect time
for saying thanks so much...

for sharing your friendship with me.

— Collin McCarty

My Friend, Thank You

Thank you for all the
    moments we've shared —
moments filled with shared
    feelings and thoughts,
dreams and wishes,
    secrets, laughter and tears,
and above all, friendship.
Each precious second will be treasured
    in my heart forever.

Thank you for taking time —
time to stop and take an interest in me;
time to listen to my problems
    and help me find the solutions,
and most of all,
time to smile at me and show you care.

Thank you for being you —
   you're a wonderful person.
You were there when
I needed you to confide in
   and to ask advice from.
Through you, I began
   to understand
and even like myself.

How can I ever tell you
   how much I care for you?

Thank you, my friend.

— Linda Scharnhorst

I Am So Grateful
that We're Friends

I'm so thankful that we're friends,
that we can laugh together
and open our hearts to each other.
Your warmth is a special joy to me;
your understanding gives me strength.

I'm so grateful that we're friends,
that we can help each other
through the rough times with
kind words and honest caring.

Your inner beauty shines brightly;
your smile is cherished in my heart.

You are wonderful to me,
and I thank you for bringing
your love and friendship into my life.

— Donna Levine Small

Our Friendship
Will Always Be Important to Me

Do you remember the first time we met?
It seemed we came together
in instant friendship.
We somehow knew we could lean upon
  each other,
    depend upon one another.
It seemed as though we had always
been friends.

As time has gone by, those feelings
have grown.
We have shared our most secret thoughts
and dreams.

We've helped each other through times
when we never thought we could endure,
and shared with each other the
most memorable days of our lives.

For as long as I live,
you will always hold a place inside me.
Our friendship will always be
a very important part of my life.
Our relationship is very unique;
it always has been.
I look forward to our future
and to our continued sharing as friends.

— Alice Kasten

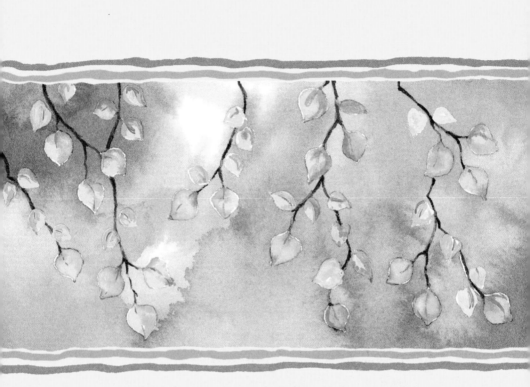

I'm Your Friend, and I'm Here if You Need Me

I can see you struggling right now.
Things that were once familiar to you
    have changed,
leaving you to feel a little lost
    and worried.
Life challenges us to grow
by putting us in different situations.
But if things seem too difficult,
remember I'm your friend.
You mean a lot to me,
and I'm here if you need me.

— Donna Levine Small

You, My Friend, Are Truly
One of Life's Gifts

Friends are one of life's gifts,
    and I have a good friend in you.
We are bonded by the growth we have shared
    over the years that we have known each other.
With each year that has passed,
    we have grown even closer.
We've loved each other through illness,
    despair, and so much more.
Together we have celebrated our youth.
With you, I have learned to laugh at myself.
You have filled my heart and mind with enough
    memories to last a lifetime.
My love for you has gone beyond friendship;
    you are a part of my family.
May the future bring us both the joy of success
and a continuing friendship to get us through
    the hard times ahead.

— L. A. Dixon

You Give Me So Much More than Friendship

You are someone who cries for me,
worries for me, and smiles for me,
and someone I can do the same for.
You are always there when I
especially need a friend,
and you let me be there for you.
You are someone who cares about me
no matter what I do or say.
You are kind, considerate, and gentle,
the type of person I look up to.
You are someone who is loving,
understanding, and compassionate,
who is easy to like and care about.
You have given so much to me:
a friendship that will last
through years and challenges,
a caring and sharing
that I treasure.
You are someone wonderful;
you are my closest friend.

— Rena Lyn Wardall

A Friendship like Ours
Is Forever

It is rare
that you meet someone
who with that first smile
becomes your friend
Someone who knows
nothing about you one day
and all your secret thoughts
the next
Someone who asks for nothing
in return for friendship
but friendship itself
Someone who makes it
just as easy to share sadness
as it is to share joy
I found that rare someone
when I found you
And like a precious memory
a friendship like ours is forever

— Dawn M. Miller

You're a Friend for All the Seasons of My Life

Through the seasons of our lives,
     friends come and go.
Some stay longer than others.
Some touch us,
     and then are gone.
But as the seasons change,
I am reassured to know
     you will always be there.
Because no matter how busy
our lives become,
our friendship remains true.
And knowing I have
the kind of friend
     I have in you
gives me new hope
to face all my tomorrows.

— Leslie J. Snodgrass

You Are So Very Important to Me

I've brought to you my insecurities
and laid them carefully around you,
hoping that you would deal
   with them gently.
You stood beside me
when so many have walked away.
You sheltered me
with affection and I felt more secure.
You did not treat me
   with insignificance,
but you showed me a brighter side,
and helped me make corrections
   along the way.
You hold a vital role in my life,
and I wanted you to know.
There are so many times when I forget
to tell you just how important
you are to me.

— Sherrie L. Householder

My Friend, You Are a Unique and Rare Individual Who Is Very Precious to Me

You're a very special friend to me.

And I really cherish
all the wonderful qualities you have:
the ones that shine so bright
for everyone to see,
and the more personal ones... that are
only known to the lucky people
who are close to you.

You've got so many good things going for you.
And the more I know of this world
and the people in it,
the more I know that you're really one of a kind.

I think I could search the world over
and never find
a more wonderful friend than you.

— Chris Gallatin

A Long-Time Friend Is One of Life's Most Precious Blessings

One nice thing about getting older
is that our friends get older, too,
    and more dear.
For there are few things in life
as precious as a long-time friend.
There's a feeling of comfort
that can't be put into words,
a sense of warmth and fulfillment
that few things in life can equal.
So here I am getting older,
    and loving it,
if only because I know that
there is someone just like me
who has been a part of my life
    for so long,
who understands me,
who remembers the "good old days,"
and who is happy to be my long-time,
lifetime friend.

You, my friend, are that special
    someone...
You are one of life's
    most precious blessings.

— Rhoda-Katie Hannan

I'll Always Remember, Dear Friend, the Moments We've Shared

We've shared some very special moments
    together:
hours of enjoyment, filled with love,
because they were spent with you.
And no matter where our paths
may lead us,
my heart and my mind will always
remember and cherish
each moment we've shared.
I will forever cherish what I
have learned from you.
And one thing is certain:
I will never ever forget you
as long as I live,
for you have left your imprint
on my heart
and your presence in my soul.
I'll love you forever, dear friend,
no matter what the future brings.
I'll always remember
our special moments together.

— Jane Alice Pedersen

As I look back on all that's happened
    between you and me —
growing up, growing together,
changing you, changing me —
there were times
when we dreamed together,
when we laughed and cried together.
As I look back on those days,
I realize how much I truly miss you
and how much I truly loved you.
The past may be gone forever...
and whatever the future holds,
our todays make the memories of tomorrow.
So, my lifetime friend,
it is with all my heart
that I send you my love,
hoping that you'll always carry my smile
    with you,
for all we have meant to each other,
and for whatever the future may hold.

— C. L. Purdy

Who knows what the future holds?
Anything can happen —
we may be together,
we may drift apart.
Yet no matter what happens,
I'll always have warm thoughts of you.
And I know in my heart that
in the future, no matter where I go,
what I'm doing, or who I'm with,
there is one thing I can assure you of:
at any given moment,
should a memory of you flash
　　through my mind
or if, for any reason, I should
　　find myself thinking back to you,
there will always be
　　a smile on my face.

— Lynn Barnhart

My Friend,
Know in Your Heart that
I Am Always with You

When true friendship
binds two individuals together,
that bond can never be broken.
For in times of confusion,
I will be there to listen to you.
In times of sadness,
I will be there to console you.
In times of anger,
I will be there to talk with you.
Even when miles separate us,
   my friend,
when you are confused,
when you are sad,
when you are angry,
search your heart,
and I will be there.
I am and always will be
your friend.

— Joel Delizo

Maybe You Can Do This
Special Favor for Me, My Friend

For the times when
    we're apart,
I want you to keep me in your heart
    and in your mind.

Just quietly close your eyes once in a while
and imagine me here, smiling and thinking
    such thankful thoughts of you.

For I spend so many quiet moments
    of my own
thinking how much I miss you,
    and how hard it is to be apart,

and how wonderful it is
that you're always with me,
warm and cherished...
    here in my heart.

— A. Rogers

I Hope We Will
Always Be Special Friends

A special friend is a rare find...
someone who shares your joy
and happiness,
someone who cares enough
to show love and kindness,
someone who is a comfort
to spend time with,
someone who is honest
and thoughtful.

A special friend is a wonderful gift...
someone who offers understanding
when life is difficult,
someone whose smile is enough
to brighten any day,
someone who accepts you
and is glad that you are you,
someone who forgets mistakes
and is gentle and trusting.

You are this special friend to me.
Our times together are
treasured in my heart.
I wish you love, laughter,
and all of life's
most beautiful things.
I wish you health and cheer,
and more of everything
that makes you happy.
And I wish that we will
always be special friends.

— Donna Levine Small

I've Been Thinking About You,
My Friend

When you read these words,
chances are that I'll be sitting here
thinking of you...
as I so often do.
I'll probably be smiling
one of the smiles that I always do
when thoughts of you come my way.

When you read these few words,
I hope you'll think,
just for a moment,
how much you mean to me
and how much you always will.

And when you continue on with the things
you need to be doing in your day,
smile a smile for me, and remember

that I'll be thinking of you still.

— A. Rogers

True Friends Always Remain in Each Other's Heart

A friend is someone who listens without judging you — right or wrong, good or bad — and gently helps you define your thoughts to regain perspective.

When you're feeling bad about yourself, a friend is there to remind you of all those positive qualities you may have forgotten.

When you share with a friend, decision making becomes easier and problems seem less critical.

A friend gives you the priceless gift of time: time to share, to try out new ideas, and to rethink old ones. No matter how often you're together, you discover dimensions of yourself through the bonds and the mirror of friendship.

A friend loves you for who you are, not what you do. Feeling so accepted, you are able to set higher goals, try harder, and achieve more.

Through close friendship, you learn the fine art of giving. You expand, become more selfless, feel more deeply, and help more effectively. Seeing the happiness you bring to another person gives you a greater sense of well-being and increases your capacity to love.

Wherever you go in life, whatever stage or place you reach, a friend who has entered your soul is always with you, gently guiding, faithfully following, and ever walking beside you.

— Sandra Sturtz Hauss

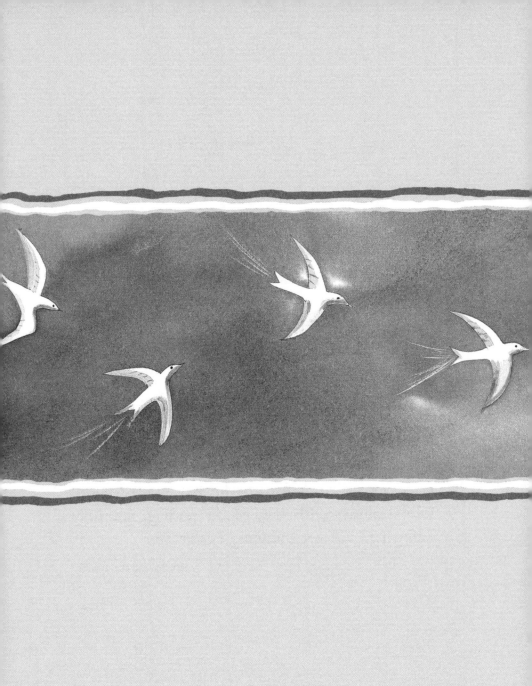

I Can't Wait to Be
with You Again, My Friend

When we are apart
sometimes a phone call
or a letter
can bring us so close
that I can see
you by my side
but as soon as
we are done talking
or I am finished reading
your letter
I realize once again
the distance that
  separates us
I think about all
that we have shared
and I miss seeing you
and I can't wait
to be with you again

— Susan Polis Schutz

To a Friend
Who Is Dear to Me

There are certain people who we are
so close to and who are
so dear to our hearts
There are certain people who can
bring us a ray of happiness
with just a smile
and who can make us feel better
just by listening and showing
that they care
There are certain people who can
make our day with a kind word
They can bring us hope when
our hearts are low
They are a part of who we are
and they make a difference in our lives
They offer us the comfort of knowing
someone understands
and the satisfaction of knowing
we have something to believe in

It's special friendships like these
that provide us with
a sense of security
These special kinds of friends are
treasured within the heart and are
a part of our souls
They offer words of wisdom
with their advice
and they heal broken hearts
just by being there to listen
They are people like you
who are so deserving
of such admiration and praise...
for it's friends like you who are
forever loved so dearly

— Shannon M. Lester